Words are mechanical—they have functions—imaginations and brilliancies. In *Light Wind Light Light*, Bin Ramke seems intent on transcending the notion of "single use"—his poems expand fractically, rhizomatically, in multiple dimensions and qualities. I have long thought of him as one of those poets working in the lyric mode who mistrusts that tendency of the lyric to tie off all its loose ends; in Ramke's book the "lyric" is music—its desire is not to fix a position but to echo, to resound. Rather than argument, invitation and engagement are the rhetoric in play.

Kazim Ali // *Sky Ward*

Ardent and indelible, spare as the bones of a bird, these artifacts of an acute sensibility are sparked by the resurgent memories of infancy: forest and bees, river and fish, storm and rain, puddle and sky—all this of no consequence; all this of vital significance.

I was the child there watching.

Rikki Ducornet // *Brightfellow*

These poems contain the curves, ratios, relations, laws, and forces that describe existence and bind thing to thing, the fact of which, we might say, constitutes reality: self to word, law to light or sun or moon, wind to breath, not just physically but also through the furthering force of metaphor. In this world, all surfaces are in intimate communication, inviting us to "[walk] out to be there breathless" amidst its glorious connections. Ramke's gift, given to the reader again and again, is in how he traces the fragility and glow of living movement, like gold coursing through thought.

Eleni Sikelianos // *Make Yourself Happy*

light wind light light

Also by BIN RAMKE:

The Difference Between Night and Day // Yale University Press // 1978
White Monkeys // University of Georgia Press // 1981
The Language Student // Louisiana State University Press // 1986
The Erotic Light of Gardens // Wesleyan University Press // 1989
Massacre of the Innocents // University of Iowa Press // 1995
Wake // University of Iowa Press // 1999
Airs, Waters, Places // University of Iowa Press // 2001
Matter // University of Iowa Press // 2004
Tendril // Omnidawn Publishing // 2007
Theory of Mind: New & Selected Poems // Omnidawn Publishing // 2009
Aerial // Omnidawn Publishing // 2012
Missing the Moon // Omnidawn Publishing // 2014

LIGHT
WIND
LIGHT
LIGHT

OMNIDAWN PUBLISHING
OAKLAND, CALIFORNIA
2018

Cover art by Moira McDonald: "Origami Boat," Unique lumen photograph (8"x10").
I wanted to make a photograph of how it feels to be floating in a river. So I made an
origami boat and as it went down stream, it also made this picture.
www.moiramcdonald.com

Back cover photo by jenelle stafford. www.jeneldorado.com

Text set in Century Gothic & Garamond 3 LT Std

Cover & Interior Design by Sharon Zetter

Offset printed in the United States
by Edwards Brothers Malloy, Ann Arbor, Michigan
On 55# Enviro Natural 100% Recycled 100% PCW
Acid Free Archival Quality FSC Certified Paper

Library of Congress Cataloging-in-Publication Data

Names: Ramke, Bin, 1947- author.
Title: Light wind light light / Bin Ramke.
Description: Oakland, California : Omnidawn Publishing, 2018. | Includes
    bibliographical references.
Identifiers: LCCN 2017051244 | ISBN 9781632430533 (pbk. : alk. paper)
Classification: LCC PS3568.A446 A6 2018 | DDC 811/.54--dc23
LC record available at https://lccn.loc.gov/2017051244

Published by Omnidawn Publishing, Oakland, California
www.omnidawn.com   (510) 237-5472   (800) 792-4957
10 9 8 7 6 5 4 3 2 1
ISBN: 978-1-63243-053-3

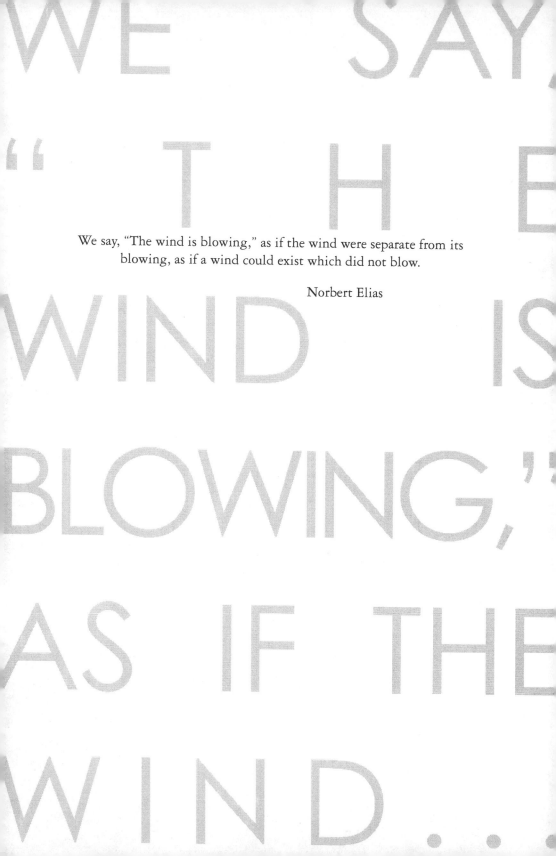

We say, "The wind is blowing," as if the wind were separate from its blowing, as if a wind could exist which did not blow.

Norbert Elias

what may not itself be touched in turn can never touch.

Lucretius

for Linda and Nic

CONTENTS

•

Words as Wind, and Wind // 19
Animals Imagined // 20
The Brouwer Fixed-Point Theorem // 21
The Thing Itself // 22
On Paper // 23
Conventional Language // 24
Navigational Chart // 25
Beneath Is Better (A Theory of Understanding) // 27
Forest Bees // 29
The Great Wave of Kanagawa // 30
Port Royal Logic // 31
Another End // 32
The Law, the Other Law (Jury Duty) // 33

• •

Wind, Winding, Wind // 38
Saturn's Rings Are a Sign of Remorse // 39
Theodicy for Beginners // 40
Fall. Things. Sudden (I) // 42
The World Vibrates Variously // 44
Fall. Things. Sudden (II) // 46
What Was Thought Then // 47
The Robe of Ephod, All of Blue // 48
On Pleasure // 51
The Year Light Became Visible // 52
Precarious (Obtained By Prayer) // 54
The Light of the Blue Sun Blazes // 55
Visible Is What Others Are Not What I Can Do // 56
White Horse Asterism // 59
My Chinese Name // 61
Spider Mind // 62

Witness (The Modern Sublime) // 66
Body Felt // 69
Isolating Splendor // 70
Learning Light from Dark // 71
Tree Names and Folk Etymology // 73
To Save Spider and Fly Alike // 74
In the Far South the Sun of Autumn Is Passing // 75
Atmospheric Perspective // 79
Louisiana, Then // 80
Enclosure // 81
Windfarm Wind // 82
A Map of My Lesser Years // 83
The Past the Passing // 84

● ● ● ●

Afterward: On *Light Wind Light Light* // 89

Notes & Acknowledgments // 91

Sources // 93

·

...we find no vestige of a beginning,
—no prospect of an end

James Hutton (1788)

WORDS AS WIND, AND WIND

Across the sound the sound
and soiled water whisked. What we miss we who live
late against the mountains, high desiccant,
we miss misery of a sort, we miss

wet seasonal surges. I have a gate here
and a wall and plants planted and a path.
I have a plan to ignore. I plant.
I seethe against the seed-eating avian,
I pluck beetles by hand to drown in soap.

What makes a garden is a gate. What makes
a gate is a fence—otherwise it is a trellis,
I do love a trellis, and a morning glory.

There was an early morning I was awake and the storm
had a name and the storm stopped, sudden as waking,
and I walked out to be there breathless but as if

being breathed myself, a wet wind from
a sleeping mouth,
and then the storm blew opposite
itself like passengers on a train talking.

ANIMALS IMAGINED

A boy on a horse,
a boy on a horse along a river.
Less simple—time intervenes thievish.
A boy on a horse in the rain along a river.
A picture emerges from mist—faint rain
hiding the regnant risk, arrowing rain,
boy lost on a horse in the rain along a river,
a high bluff beside water. Story:
the bit firm in the horse's mouth
the hand of the boy unfirm.
What we played we played, dangerous
only in retrospect.
If it can be remembered
it was survived,
the era of imagined
horses in radiant landscape;
only the rivers remain.

THE BROUWER FIXED-POINT THEOREM

I took a map of my home town
and crumpled it into folds
of cerebellum. Sixty years later
I superimposed it onto the living
place, the city of this moment.

Imagine I am stirring coffee watching
a single still-point memorious:
a bulls-eye around which whirls
dark movement. Imagine

I am alive upon this plane
where birds and insects
chase each other. Children devour parents.
Roses petal and perfume.
Beetles gleam green
against forests after eating entire
coats of cambium beneath the bark.

THE THING ITSELF

Peter Hobson said the autistic
child accepts an object as object,
does not insist it be part of some other;
can sit with a found wheel to spin
for hours not pretend
he steers a boat.

Respect for what is is disease.

ON PAPER

What does it matter—*material* as in
paper, scissors, rock? Matter of fact,
res facti, not matter of law; *res judicata*;
mater, wood, in the woods, mother; a
child draws a box, triangle, chimney,
door of paper. A poem a product
suitable for interior use—hollow,
with corrugated support; or a
writing on paper from some wasp's nest

A game is played to determine matters
beyond law, beneath it: paper covers rock.
Words for "write" in most languages
have a violent origin—cut, scratch,
incise. A few were painterly. To write
in water. To write in sand. To make
a house of paper, a floating.
Writan, to tear, as paper, skin, cloth.

CONVENTIONAL LANGUAGE

Things that can be opened:
old wounds, old wines,
envelopes, books,
frontiers.

Oh, and eyes.

My mother, born the year her language
became illegal, opened doors
to secret water. She spoke in spite,
closing or disclosing at will.

"Cajun French ... did not begin its demise
until the 20th century, with the advent of
compulsory schooling in English in 1916."

NAVIGATIONAL CHART

(Rebbilib) Marshall Islands, Coconut Midrib Fiber
19th- Early 20th Century

Amid the museum susurrus
I was startled by wicker
strips tied into flat patterns,
a graph on three axes, mappings
of water and wind over time
sensed disruptions
in currents by
navigators of patterns felt
among islands—

the flimsiest boat is beautiful
when someone survives.

It is said that a fisherman would study his charts, leave them behind,
and then lie on his back in the canoe, the better to feel the rise and fall
of the ocean swells. He interpreted the map with his body memory,
not with his eyes.   Suzanne Fierston

not to drown is not enough,
but is a start.

Who sleeps on water
not in water—
contained by light
(fishermen warned us fish could see
our shadows)

I slept on a river surface
the boat would resound
and rise as boats passed, a knocking of waves
against us not to be feared because

we had permanent mooring,
a deadman held us fast.
The water flexed and we floated
safely stopped, static, home.

I was the child there watching
birds watch fishy shadows
on the surface—I could not see
down as they did, but I could see
them seeing into depths.
I felt the waves from passing boats
like code, in Morse for mariners.

I once took the wheel, my uncle standing
behind me, of a tugboat on the Mississippi;
the wheel taller than I was but I could see
the water and traffic afloat; I felt trembling
in my startling hands.

BENEATH IS BETTER
(A THEORY OF UNDERSTANDING)

wings of angels rustle in Latin
says Zbigniew Herbert

I recall so little (*amo amas
amat*) the little so broken I
sauntered soundless
down paths in the park

I heard a policeman speak
in fragments from above

from a helicopter I understood
little

less than Latin

rotors and engines and roaring traffic
a soup of grammars and syntax

Angel is an ancient word for
Entropy which word was invented
in 1868 by Clausius

I mean the turning inward
downward
demanded by police

Energy is another word another
world at night a bird

probably mockingbird

keeps awake
the weary

means nothing by it
"Means"
"Nothing"

entropia, turning inward
an older word

than the French for *Cajun*
acadienne but

perspective was invented by Vitruvius
then was not needed until
the invention of the railroad in 1789
by William Jessup who
invented the wheel
or a flanged version of it
to hang onto an iron rail

I learned from a book there are
trees beneath earth

Geoxylic suffrutices
forests sunk

trunks underground
and the merest wisp
of leaves left visible

within earth beneath fire
beneath breath of man or cosmos
immortal wooden wilderness.

FOREST BEES

is how I first read his name, Forrest
Bess, a neighbor

(Varroa, mites on bees, bite;
bees may evolve resistance;
mites may evolve avirulence—a parasite
keeps its efforts less than fatal
so host and parasite thrive together

is one definition of art);

feral bees of the forest returning
form a figure against the light at evening;

figure might be a number or a nude;

an erotic calculus was my goal, boundary,
like the edge of a forest the drawing
assumes—in that era bees belonged to us
yet would escape and strew
honey in hollowness.

THE GREAT WAVE OF KANAGAWA

Hokusai noticed a wave
waving in which the particulate sea became birds—flung
spray flew toward mountains.

This is not true. Clearly the siege of white cranes
lies behind the wave, not of it. And yet. It is all
paper for the folding.

PORT ROYAL LOGIC

We were speaking, she and I, of measure theory—
or we were not, but could have been—anything
would have served. To speak, to form a space
within which to touch, to nearly touch, to try.

I have spoken of the agonies I took
learning to write 5, but equally
I worked toward the satisfactory 2
with all curves reversing—still

learning to draw rockets to carry me
and occasional ships of the sea subject
to this unsteady hand;

today above my house a new cloud boils into view
all bubbles and curves. Analytic airs.

ANOTHER END

as in *purpose*; the purple of the hillside
enrolled me in its misery, mysterious mist
emanating.

       When it was over the day
descended in the form of a star, ours,
which is to say the dark returned

which is to say a measure of darkness inter-
posed between and among the sources
the lights twinkling against a moon.

This was a landscape longed for, lost.
Long as a verb—to increase in length
of days, of nights, of neither.

Still the purple stain, floral embellishment,
ingrains itself, inhabits banished gardens.

THE LAW, THE OTHER LAW (JURY DUTY)

Plato said the world is a body of fire so we can see and
of earth so we can touch, but we cannot touch.

LAWLESS

When I was a child we would go to the movies
whenever; we would buy our tickets and find seats
then when we recognized where we were in the
story we would leave—"this is where we came in."

The path of the planet Venus against the sky
a slow act of vision, not rare:
who has not seen in part, without recognition,
without knowing where he came in? Even
the blind can see, slowly enough.

Pretend the earth doesn't move
let Venus make circles around us
a shape repeatable; after eight years
a lovely path five-pointed
out of a mesh of angles emerges.

        //

A theory of evidence
under the law: Words are mine
neither before nor after I say them;

words are mine when the saying occurs.
"Words" is wrong. "Sentences" is better
but wrong. No to *ideas*. No to *things*.
"Poems." That works, members of the jury:
every witness a poet.

A problem: the man
before you is not the boy who did it.
The Greeks (Aristotle) had two words
for number. One for amounts, one
for quantity: how much, how many.

Time is a kind of number, a number
of change with respect to before
and after. Before the event he was
foolish; after, he was guilty. In any
garden this morning are caterpillars
which in weeks will be butterflies.

We are accuser and accused. We listen
and speak. My now is not your now.

OTHER LAW

In *Timaeus* we learn the planets
were made to stand guard over
the numbers of time.

You saw the shape of the path of Venus
in the sky—the apparent shape of a line
it drew against the sky—a dashed line
of light in the night, brightly
held in the eye for years.

(If ripe fruit never falls he is still innocent.)

Seven days and seven years are the same
number. Seven dogs and seven mountains
are the same number. We notice time

when we notice change. (*Arithmos*, number,
metron, measure.) Tears can be counted,
weight of water can be measured.

//

Instruction Number One
The elements of the crime of murder
in the first degree are:
(1) that the defendant
(2) at and triable in the city of _____, state of_____,
    on or about the date charged
(3) after deliberation, and with intent
(4) To cause the death of a person other than himself,
(5) caused the death of another.

We think there has been time
whenever the soul says that nows
are two. The accused is one, now.

//

Guilt is a privilege of leisure.
Astronomy is a nostalgia,
one of many—consider the care
with which one must look,
the way we mark movement
of those little lights against
the dark, the pattern intricating.

To say *this is where I came in*
asserts the right to leave.

• •

The marionette, being "real life," is easily accessible. Everyone understands the marionette whether it's walking or dancing or fighting We can see it and it makes sense. But watch instead the hands of the puppeteers. Can you look at the hand movements of the puppeteers and know what the marionette is doing?

Piper Alexis Harron

WIND, WINDING, WIND

Solar wind
has large effects on the tails of comets
small effects on ships
through space. A place such as

the earth once had ten suns, each in turn
shone upon us. One time all ten appeared
and would have destroyed us but
for the archer Hou Yi

who shot down nine suns. Another day
Hou Yi stole the elixir of life
and would have ruled earth
but for his wife, Chang'e,

who drank the elixir then floated
to the moon—because Hou Yi loved Chang'e
he did not shoot down the moon.

The Chinese space program's
Chang'e 2 arrived at the moon October 6, 2010.
The name is spelled variously in English.

    //

We listened to the recording
of a man asking for help;
it was the past, we knew he would not get it,
that it would be worse than that.

We could hear the gun fired,
and his voice even as he said
thank you to the policeman on the telephone.

SATURN'S RINGS ARE A SIGN
OF REMORSE

Further study of the solar wind
involved: Wind, ACE, and SOHO satellites.
To intend is not to attend but
the wind is called willful yet has no will
has only effect, and cause

wind wave waft whisper:
susurration of the planetary system

I spent one morning on Saturn
after a long week of work, I walked
under its rings, renouncing
the world I knew, believed I knew

belief is a kind of winding, a wind
of desire around a spindle of self.
Spindly self, surrounded, bounded.

THEODICY FOR BEGINNERS

The first half of the alphabet
is for known quantities: a is known,
b is known, a + b = x
the second half of the alphabet
is for unknown quantities
solve for x delta y over delta x
as x approaches zero...

//

We did watch the cloud-colored moon
against the night-colored night.
The moon is where night lives
one night every month.

We watched the sky-colored cloud
that morning from the airport, through
the acres of glass the wall
where one airline's swift
passengers waited for the first
flight out of the day. The day
was the color of the sky-colored
clouded sun rising into spectacle.

We were all preparing to tread
on air, to use the weight of air
on earth against gravity.

//

The world consists of objects,
properties and relations,
functions and propositions.
Eyes can be closed. Hands
opened.

//

The work of our hands when we have
hands; we spend our days as a tale
that is told, completed before ending. So
while we wait we make things, small
things that click or sing to us. Crickets
of straw and string. Plucked.

Another thing to do is to think
but the glitter of horizon
casts bright shadows against us
thus we must watch closer
think more finely like children

even though the number of our days
diminishes, like light like little toys
made of leftover light.

FALL. THINGS. SUDDEN (I)

To know better—

Paul on the road struck down by light
never the same again. I crossed the street
myself to be struck by a careless car
and after plastic surgery was the same.

    //

"Assume any relation betwixt x and z that you please"
    Isaac Newton

Subitize: know the number immediately
without counting;
usually three or less, but arrangement
can enable a higher non-counting knowledge.

"*Litost* (Czech), a state of agony and torment created by
the sudden sight of one's own agony and torment"

    //

During my first semester of college one Sunday I, aware
of the time, sat talking to a girl, wary. I usually attended
mass by noon but there was a later one I could go to.
The talking continued and the hours passed and at a
certain moment I knew I would not be attending the
services. And I rather curiously knew also I would
never again attend the services, I who had been the
best of good Catholic boys, who had never eaten meat
on Friday nor missed mass on Sunday.

And it was a kind of nothing, of no consequence.
It was autumn, the best of all seasons in Baton Rouge
made livable by live oaks and late magnolias blooming.

THE WORLD VIBRATES VARIOUSLY

Yet is mainly made of wood and
bark (noun) barking (verb),
could be called Yggdrasil

a bird at night mocking sings
to keep me awake
when I need to dream
to sleep I am elsewhere
when I hear a policeman speak
from above and understand
the sound of rotors; the traffic
noise has its own grammar
syntactical energy dispensing
the wisdom of wind.

        //

Sometimes we must make do with
illustration: "The Farm Near Duivendrecht"
a painting of reflection for instance since
(Nature loves to hide)
said Heraclitus

        //

Eventually lines align into geometry,
cleanly. Clearly Mondrian meant to salvage
the world, as do we all. I, too, loved his later works
only after learning to see through paint;
what I mean to say is
any meaning brings its own violence,
art as ark, as a cleansing symmetry sells.
(see *Plastic Mathematics* (Schoenmaekers)

The story cannot be told in profane language
in a dirty world reflecting itself
in every puddle every sky
bounding and bouncing light back
at us (*Observing sea, sky, and stars,*
I sought to indicate their plastic function
through a multiplicity of
crossing verticals and horizontals.)

back and below
where the lines converge
as the layers linger
humming along.

FALL. THINGS. SUDDEN (II)

To know how many without counting
is a curious skill. Subitizing. Usually three
or fewer but arrangement can enable
a higher non-counting knowledge:

     //

and it becomes a kind of nothing,
of no consequence. It was autumn
the best of all seasons
among great blue herons.

WHAT WAS THOUGHT THEN

A body boils with life after
the mind goes to vapor. Microbial.
A wisp arose from her body abandoned
there on the table for looking with one's
own eyes: a bit of steam in a cold
room. Molecular. One rose
by her bed back home.

An incompleteness theorem means
she could never formulate correct and complete
descriptions of the set of natural numbers.

Her life did add up: Mom. When I see
the photograph of Kurt Gödel
by Arnold Newman
I think of her death. She had been breathing long
noisy breaths then a quiet crept
behind my sister and me,
murmured beyond us as we sat.

A blackboard that was well used
is now erased. Gray dusted
wisped with a vaporous powder of chalk.

I suspect that mourn is related to murmur
we stilly watch the body lie.

THE ROBE OF EPHOD, ALL OF BLUE

I would make my new scripture I said
and it will sound reringingly against the cold
she said. We said it would work this way—
consider all instructions, Old Testament and New,
New to Modern. Follow the rules.

A golden bell and a pomegranate, a golden bell and a pomegranate,
upon the hem of the robe round about. Exodus 28:34

For glory and for beauty, a lesson in fashion
served for decisions: *thummim*, white, scissorly;
urim, black, clip, divination, answers against
unknowing, resewing: spontaneous divination
through the folds of fallen fabric, creased
linens wear into transparency

a way to know is a reason to sew—
relining my favorite jacket I laid
out the scraps to cut and inside-out re-place
the pieces...simple task for the righteous,
new linings in old jackets;

Sound. The blue robe efflorescent.

                    //

Against the cold the cleverly resewn garment
seals in the fleshwarm fervor; I said I
wanted to sound serious. (Sound, adjective)

Still the snow fell furious as ever, ever failing:
fellowship of the cold continued to disappoint.
We who could listen coldly countered, counted,
ourselves believers. Dressed warmly in fabrics.

//

What to wear what to wear. Such a blue
encourages where courage is due.

//

Here is how we would know:
through the contemplation of the petals
of the poppy, folds of fabric predict
as surely as do the dreams narcotic.

Through stepping on pages strewn
a priest of the ironing board notices
creased accidents of dress and desire
pressing and predicting.

Pecthimancy, or petchimancy: reading
a future in brushed cloth.

Wax-burning or melting or simply
staining the clothing she wore that night
can be read as revealing.

Any stoichomancy will work—a future
falls with the grace of silk, of aerophanes
to see through, of baggings and baizes,
of batiste's visual flirtations. The past
remains in brocades abraded, worn
into visual puns. To wear is to wear
no matter how carefully
we sit and stand and dance at
arm's length, she said, sadly
folding her cambresine,
eyeing her zephyrous scarves.

//

...textile conservators discovered fragments of medieval manuscripts lining the hems of dresses at the Cistercian convent of Wienhausen in Northern Germany. The dresses in question, made by nuns in the late fifteenth century, clothed the convent's statues.
        Nora Wilkinson

ON PLEASURE

Chuang Tzu said to Hui Tzu,
on the bank of the river Hao:
Observe the pleasures of the fishes, joyously splashing
against sun-light. To which Hui Tzu said:
You are no fish, you cannot know if they know pleasure.
To which Chuang Tzu said: *You are no Chuang Tzu,*
you cannot know what I know. The river spoke
but neither man nor fish could hear.

THE YEAR LIGHT BECAME VISIBLE

Medgar Evers was murdered. John Kennedy
was murdered. Sylvia Plath killed herself.
Tristan Tzara died, as did Theodore Roethke.
Thich Quang Durc killed himself. Others
died elsewhere, home and away. I
went briefly away that summer
then returned home.

For six weeks I studied analysis, least
upper bounds and greatest lower bounds,
and in the evenings how to play Go.
We made our own board
of paper and drawn lines,
with a few dollars worth of pennies
heads black, tails white
for stones. We boys and girls
of the adolescent world
of mathematics greeted
each other like foxes fleeting
shy along highways.

//

But the water surface ripples, the whole light changes.
            "The Skaters," John Ashbery

I decided to study the universe as if I lived there.
Imagined it. A visitor here myself, I made myself

at home. A Martian engulfed in his own ignorance
of water, I drank as if drowning. The gulf between us

a piece of pursuit, an area subtending
tending to disappear in the morning light of Venus

PRECARIOUS
(Obtained By Prayer)

"Self" hidden from the winding
various winds: wilderness within
is another term for it, term
as in space or time, terminus.

Reflection in however shallow a pond
completes the image, a watery,
wavering face. Momentary.

A pair of white pelicans circled
above me, their movements mimicked
each by each, searching I suppose
for water for landing (the irony)
a small pond I could point to,
they could rest.

I followed them a brisk walk across
a park but then they circled
behind a line of trees and when
I arrived they'd left. Landed
in water, terrain.

The face beneath the water
as real as anything, nothing.

THE LIGHT OF THE BLUE SUN BLAZES

Uranus, a blue-green planet might
have been named George had Herschel
been granted his wish for a sinecure
from his king. It has
seventeen named satellites. It is a system.
It might have a ring, from certain angles.

When Venus volunteers to be the morning star
earth's day ignites slowly

and I think of mornings in Georgia
when I would place coal on wood chips
in the grate to warm the house. It was
a lovely house but we reeked and wrecked
the neighborhood air. But it was cold there then.

Sometimes Sirius is the morning star
and sometimes Mercury. Astronomy is light
and warmth at a distance only.

for Linda

VISIBLE IS WHAT OTHERS ARE
NOT WHAT I CAN DO

Anemone, daughter of wind,
was believed to bloom
only in wind;

a tree in South Africa lives underground—
a few scattered leaves on short stems
visible on the sandy surface

unseen trunks and limbs and roots
writhe forever darkly

pyrogenic—mutated defense
against fire a refusal to rise into air. It is a
geoxylic suffrutex

the most beautiful tree in the world.
It is (a theory) immortal.

      //

Wind is invisible its effects reflective
of light. Some plants pollinate by wind—
anemophilous. The wind deadly but is itself
generative of an esthetic.

To study the effect of the wind upon the stars
Ottavinao Mascherino built Tower of the Winds
in 1580 in the Vatican. A star is
the light it produces. The light is
distorted by air thus wind affects the stars.

A star is light. Only light. It is not other.
It is. This is a poetics.

//

Assume a time in the universe
when no being had vision
all that happened
was dark
did happen

//

I would lie on my belly and with a small trowel
dig carefully beside the twig until I reached
a limb and I would expose to my sight to air
and light the trunk and then I would follow
root down to nothing more of wood
but earth.

//

Hasselblad 500 EL camera number 1038
one of 15 used on the lunar surface, the only
to return

//

Grüner See is a lake in Austria that dries out in fall,
is a county park in winter is
famous in its underwater version
during the spring melt. Visible through
clarity of snow melt.

Imagine here a photograph
taken through
water, of water
containing a walk, a park,
a park bench, a tree
a tree green with new leaves
glitter

//

In many photographs
especially candid portraits
interesting shadows
sometimes of the photographer
an accidental signature,
sometimes the evening elongations
of an elderly couple smiling into the Instamatic

//

I know an artist who photographs
only her own camera
crystalline structure
of lens eye air
obstruction of light

I know an artist who lives
beside the sea who hangs wet
seaweed from a device of
her own devising to which she attaches a pen
and places paper below to enable wind to draw
depictions of contingency.

I know an artist who loves this world
and makes of it a self in paint
the color of the world in air
a thin coat of air like ice
glitter
of sun.

//

(Socrates: *I cannot help feeling, Phaedrus, that writing
is unfortunately like painting; for the creations of the
painter have the attitude of life, and yet if you ask them
a question they preserve a solemn silence*)

WHITE HORSE ASTERISM

In his glabrous youth he would draw and hope
to be correct; he would see
what he thought he saw, thoughtless.

Image is picture, or is thought to be. "Albedo"
is a word of science for the measure of a moon,
but surely some artist looked and measured

whiteness, brightness, and breathed frost
into the winter night unthinkingly.

Han Gan a thousand years ago drew horses
for his living. The emperor Xuanzong commissioned him.
You can see for a small fee his work.

Baihua, white painting, a kind of discipline.

Baimiao, white drawing, without shading.

Shade is a kind of erasure. Obliteration. Ob litera.

*ekwo- "horse" (equine). In many other languages, as in English,
this root has been lost in favor of synonyms, probably via superstitious
taboo on uttering the name of an animal so important in
Indo-European religion.
http://www.etymonline.com)

We had a white horse I would ride after school
and on weekends. An old horse when we bought him
named Flash without irony, a clever horse he inhaled
as I approached with the saddle then after cinching
he breathed so the saddle loosened.

Flash of water as hooves
reluctantly pick a course across the stream, his learned

resentment like breath wafts back to me who sadly sat
watching him work, walk with iron shoes that slipped
and did sometimes spark on dry highways.

Night-shining White is the best name in the world,
astronomy the happiest study. Happy the horseless
watching Equuleus, daughter of centaur and nymph

become a dim constellation of little
importance. Who shines
with a lesser light, little splash, few
watchers, two planets. In the night.

*(The sun and moon and five other stars, which are called the planets,
were created by him in order to distinguish and preserve the numbers
of time; and when he had made their several bodies, he placed them
in the orbits in which the circle of the other was revolving,—in seven
orbits seven stars.*

*SOCRATES: Excellent, Timaeus, I like your manner of approaching
the subject—proceed.)*

MY CHINESE NAME

Singletree is a word for a system of pivots and posts to enable oxen to pull efficiently on plows and carts. Whiffletree or *whippletree* is an elaboration of the term, an elaboration of the system, used in typewriters and windshield wipers, in analog computers and IBM Selectric typewriters. In Meifu Wang's intricate mind cascades of levers release forces and emblems. A field or forest for instance. Floral sprays indicate paths where neurons encountered the love the resistance I pursued for fifty years since first trying to make of words the proofs I mathematically failed.

I wanted to make poems before I knew what such making entailed. Afterward was too late to stop. This is how everyone's life will be written: *obire*, the Latin (dead language) finite infinitive, to die. She offered to translate my writing, name included.

Identity. What is what. Does A always equal A, or is it sometimes the case that by the time the equal sign is crossed (by vision, the eye-movement required) A is else, even elsewhere?

I saw this morning a small bird peer out as if at me as if at movement that his analog analytics arranged in two columns—dangerous, not dangerous. A does not equal B. But also I was too big to eat, so she returned to her life. I admire the leaves surrounding us, the pale undersides setting off the gloss of a dark receptivity to sunlight. It was a linden, which makes a sort of dome of leafage—peering up I saw umbrellaed arrangements of sticks and leaves, levering whiffletrees keeping alive.

SPIDER MIND

my best friend was my mother and she was deliberate, clever, patient, soothing,
reasonable, dainty, subtle, indispensable, neat, and as useful as a spider
                    Louise Bourgeois

Small spiders seem
as if a boy could make them of thread, a button
and black wire. In the sun they glitter.

Large spiders seem as if
a boy could be bitten into darkness
with pain and the past. The fur
of the spider feels of poison, parental.

       //

We would find spiders dried along the baseboards
a problem to be swept

         Tell me a story she said, of dark
stars depleted into power
of nights glittering black over black
of moons manned and monitored;
of a century past, abandoned.
The king responded to long
narration with short attention. He longed
for sleep but she long
into the night awake
demanded more. Maternally more.

A machine which mimicked all
began to make a self out of itself
which other self rejoiced to be machine.

//

Every child I know knew to watch the corners
where spiders most easily web, x y z
points to place silk and map the stereo-
graphic world of insect.

       The child is small
is made of smallness to feel closer
to insect than to parent—the child
can be caught and wrapped alive blanketed
in paralytic love. (We watched a crying
comedian stand by the iron lung to spy
on the child within, victim.
A lung of steel and thread and buttons.)

//

Music can work the way
the spider works the way
of repetition, of pattern swaying
in time and breezes:
Quattro Pezzi su una nota sola
eleven Italian syllables
Four Pieces on a Single Note.
The spider with a single tool
builds her universe. The spider
with a second tool injects
her poison, extends her universe.
The spider with a third tool turns
her body into breakfast.

//

A music of one note: duplicate
arrange attend attend:
her mind is a thing. Like a button
sewn onto a toy.

．
．　．

This was science, scrupulous and firm, but doing it was an art. In the end you had to justify every move, every conclusion, but the whole argument slid forward on intuition, like an ice cube skating on its own melt.

Gregory Benford,
"Bow Shock"

WITNESS (THE MODERN SUBLIME)

What need does matter have to be witnessed by anyone?
        Levi Bryant

Like clouds
above

an alternate
self in the clouded mirror
not light but vapor
not a percentage of water
a pure trace
evanescent
an evaporative

to solve a life
dissolve
wisp

a wavery engagement
erosion at
last is vapor as if
sublimed

(passage directly from solid
to gaseous form = sublimation)

to become your own ghost
shamble into shadow

a happy adulthood
farcical
in the clattering spring
and fall flowering toward

a flowing below
a ladderly entrancing

form of cloud (rain) forming
rivers (dissolving earth) into
a humid forest of selves
populating

we do make claims to making:
"the Analytical Engine weaves
algebraical patterns
just as the Jacquard-loom weaves
flowers and leaves" said Ada Lovelace
whatever lives lives long
enough

                //

late in life
from within where
the hand manipulates
the dummy mouth
comes sly silence.

Speak up like vapor
rising from the candle
thinning three
dimensionally against
blue from
the window seat

all gone ungainly
when we deplane
grumbling against each
others' backs clutching
baggage.

In the large city
at the edge of

the lake, placid
where the child watching
and being watched
does not sing to himself:
My ship my little ship
my shape of ship in water
in air in mist in mind

for Nicolas

BODY FELT

only body but not
only other but the outer in
interior. Or removed and tossed

a snake skin found in the forest electric
translucent. ((*Who did* you *see die* said my sister
in the dark after the funeral, both of us thinking

necessary thoughts) (dreams
explain the world as (long as) you remain asleep)
Who did *she* see die so young

as that? Only one) no one ever we
said to each other each to the other.

ISOLATING SPLENDOR

The etymology of *brown* includes *bright*,
burnish gives bronze a color or only a metalish wish;

watching testimony in the sentencing phase.

Smoke disconnects itself from both
fire and fuel

I was a child running
down a reflective corridor
bright, waxed linoleum
past marble walls beneath
a ceiling defeated, fallen apart, dark
smoke-stained rafters

I heard a girl running
the flapping of the girl's skirt
an engagement of force and friction
wind
wending against the wind the wild
bird flutters few feathers

lands along the lake
I am watching reflections
of herons wading

they stab whatever shines beneath.

LEARNING LIGHT FROM DARK

"I throw a spear into the darkness. That is intuition. Then I must send
an army into the darkness to find the spear. That is intellect." "Ingmar
Bergman Confides in Students," *New York Times*, May 7, 1981

Spear— grandfather harpooned gar, primitive fish, food—a translation
of *gar: spear*
is a sleek word, a concept. Ching-chu produced
a set of five pictures in which a black ox gradually whitens then in the
fifth picture disappears. Thrown spear-like (spark)

against the future, dark against the light.
An early physicist asked, if one reaches the edge
then throws a spear where does it go: my first
morning at college I found the track to jog but watched

a woman throw the javelin. Odd word,
Celtic in origin, (the fork of a tree). Nothing is less
a fork than a javelin, straight and sleek, unambiguous.
I learned new boundaries—threw from the edge

watched the edge retreat before the sharpened point.
> *Before our eyes thing seems to limit thing,*
> *air bounds the hills and*   De Rerum
> *forest borders air, earth*   Natura
> *sea and sea earth, but add them up*
> *and nothing limits the sum.*

Such calculus confounds
yet opens a father's father's past into dreams
of sharp-pointed fish nosing hooks and thrashing
eelish into knots; knowledge of knots

not nothing, but *nature witholds the sum*
of existing things from providing a limit for itself
because she compels body to be bounded by void
and that again which is void to be bounded by body

and tonight I might again look up
what I read in the science section one Sunday
the discovery of the largest known nothing
in the universe and how a photon takes

a billion years to cross it, nothing as/is structure,
cold. Bounded by warmth.
The time it takes a streak of light to cross
the void, a love a lingering learned. Light light dark.

TREE NAMES AND FOLK ETYMOLOGY

On the moon a shadow,
the path gods followed from earth,
a shadow a tree called Katsura
connecting earth to sky.

A man made to fell this tree
trapped himself in his task forever.

(Leaves of Katsura resemble leaves
of the Judas tree, *Cercis siliquastrum*
from which Judas Iscariot hanged himself
early Saturday, April 4, 33AD.)

The shadow on the moon is not
the shadow of the moon, yet sisters
and brothers see from different continents
the same moon called *consolation*.

TO SAVE SPIDER AND FLY ALIKE

The conflicted world devised
       the diligence of spider to try

the trust of the rest of us. Gentle
       in her swaying self-expressed

trap spends carnivorous days in
       summer filled with flesh

(gossamer days and
       dangerous to the small).

Little lasts nothing lingers long—
       if a life is measurable it is

dying. Then done. Some flies alight
       on carrion, some on dung,
          the lucky ones.

IN THE FAR SOUTH THE SUN OF AUTUMN IS PASSING

i
Like decorations in a cemetery
poems depart part
place, hard tranquility in the face

ii
of human the sun
is distant and a source

iii
I was a child there in a previous
century's cemetery. I said three times
that word, would cringe and try

iv
"Not to die a parish death" but die
he did, I will, with some words spoken,
some not. The human is a harrowing

v
of evanescence: "the simplest words":
it is too cold for work now in the fields
the southern fields full of folk.

vi
A future emerges out of the past except
the first future. Like the last past it lives
alone, aloof. This is a way of speaking.

vii
Fat philosophers accuse themselves—judge
the past as innocent, the future so guilty
the differences narrow like a strait gate.

viii

But it could be cold there, in autumn,
even if I never saw snow but only this
ice in the effigy of fern. Frond.

ix

I would blow my breath on fingertips
to keep feeling unfrozen preparing
to touch some brown leaf, blade.

x

The face of the blackbird is a city face.
An eye that moves, a cheek that glistens
but not with tears.

xi

"Poetry is a finikin thing of air
That lives uncertainly and not for long
Yet radiantly beyond much lustier blurs."

xii

The making of the poem should be unlike
the schoolboy punished by writing
the word a thousand times.

xiii

The forbidden word. Evil the gesture.
The dark face of the mother, the sin
less than greater than gone. Never gone.

xiv

Repetition into
a meandering across a field fallow
and dry in the winds of autumn.

xv

Field shaped like a continent
emptied pillow case
fluttering white in the autumn sun weakly.

xvi

"Earth is a waxen cell of the world comb"
(Jean Toomer) Earth its own grave
its own far-off farmyard flower.

xvii

Rachel Eliza Griffiths:
"like blood
from the depths of its slight wound."

xviii

Out of the earth endlessly. With
end unavailable. Or, with end looming
always, threat of zero zeroing

xix

out of the soul, sand, salt. Out
out, a light. External
eternal lining the pathways of the park.

xx

Africa is a continent shaped like a leaf—
a leaf formed and filled with
its past leafmeal lying.

xxi

Data. Things. Dotted ground
of graves to be read redly by eyes
of grieving gods (the family survives)

xxii

Mardi Gras day when the spirits still
encased in flesh flaunt promised death
by wearing themselves colorfully.

xxiii

Symmetrical cemetery—a street lit
at night, flambeaux. Did I love
the city or the girl within it?

xxiv

A grave is of earth
out of which arises little blood
less flesh more mere spirit, poof.

xxv

A season named for
leafage, cyclical, detached,
surface resurgent.
Fall. All fallen.

ATMOSPHERIC PERSPECTIVE

A fog in the field where horses graze, grass
and cows are the route out from chaos;
gas dooms us who believe and breathe
scents and sense give us this day

which rises flame-like
as breath and absolution.

Another version: I listen
to my own breath, meditate
to slow the processes; oxygen gathers
in follicles as a vision of cows
wading through fog, cows consuming

and in the distance rising vaporous
slow as mountains, fast as food, fodder
akin to clarity. Charity. Distance.

LOUISIANA, THEN

I was a child in dust appalled:
the backward spiral of an antlion—
monstrous creature seldom

seen whole: Myrmeleontida larva whose conical
pit in sand determined a boundaried
life (ant death tiny horror)
the weight of the ant its own doom—

bound as in homeward or fastened
or the edges beyond which games cease:

back home walls of our city glittered
broken bottles set in cement
to discourage neighbors,

a city of walls and traps for visitors—
food and children plying
streets for coins; we had a river

our river its own world its waters
we drank and rode and tossed trash
into: it was us, past and passing.

ENCLOSURE

an X in a sky, contrails

against which from my place
I see five Canadian geese cross

from one park in this city
to another park in this city

"park" and "garden" words
first about walls borders

against predation the sky
open and is only light yet

is a barrier I cannot see stars
I only see these birds which

used to migrate now commute
a park was once a game preserve

a garden once a fortress.
A cloud contains itself

even a cloud of dust, even
writing itself against the light.

for Richard Ramke

WINDFARM WIND

Digital cloud twins entwine
parameters passing
yardangs on Mars show
which way the winds blew
when there was wind

thus turbulence;
thought: surface ring,
as in gyrus rectus
a map sheet, paper version
of, for instance, brain. Or planet.

It is not the wind that is farmed
it is electricity undefinable
harvested from the movements
particles and parts
thought like light like
clouds passing into /out of vision.

We do not see wind we see
what was windblown wind formed.
Birds do die but did live.

A MAP OF MY LESSER YEARS

We wrote of the facefulls of wind
which would gnaw

the space
which wind fills readily again

space is not place but
is the possibility:

a twig in the sand then
crayon on rough paper

later with blue school ink
through a Parker medium nib

on lined paper I drew rockets
clipper ships, small whales

and large dogs smiling. And
windows against wind

the wind a group of lines leaning
against trees. A shape of trees.

THE PAST THE PASSING

...for Ptolemy, whatever one thinks of him, was not useless to Copernicus.

It is a world of weather
matter and means,
and meaning itself
enough or all
especially to the vireo
watching the feeder feeding
the house finch first.

The difference between "enough" and "all" is rarely
lovely unless a leisure intervenes, a watcher not
himself lacking, missing, his measure of feed this morning.

A sun is there
even a moon
as if against
the blue appearance
of sunlight scattered
material and
relationship.

Now the sound of wings wakens the sparrows
and the cedar waxwings waft into view, onto feeders
the frenzy follows. Soon the plenty is past.

    //

The clever-footed bird builds but does not plan
I think. Climbing inside the chimney with clay
in her beak she places pieces into a shape called nest.

To cleave. Attach. Or split. Kleben or Klieben.
Cleaves clay from clay, cleaves clay to brick
a swallow's home aside from thin air luminiferous.

There is no bird whose nest hovers in air
the name of that bird is not swift, Swift
is the name of a bird who lives on air in air

ten months she sleeps in air on air she slips
downward to darkness. Is it
harder to think than to fly, happier?

A Dynamical Theory of the Electric and Luminiferous
Medium which was not so long ago the belief in light
needing a place not to rest to ride

but now we believe light needs nothing and speeds
faster in nothing than in anything. *Phoresy* is a word
about something riding on something. Cowboys

are phoresic. What a world that was, childhood
among the cows and sandhill cranes, the water the water.
I was borne by horses across narrow water.

               //

Is it the same to care and to carry? Consider Christopher
saint who never was, who did not carry the Christ
child across water which was heavy, the child heavier

by the moment then the staff he carried leafed,
leafed and fruited on the shore as sign
signal and assurance that the miraculous—another

word for mimesis—did occur once
the same man crossed the river twice.
Rejoice that water moves and mirrors indifferently.

               //

Phosphorescence is lovely to say, to feel against
tongue and teeth, air crossing the lips with force:
the choreography of a single word, a bird

landing on one twig amid a twirl of twigs winded.
Light-bearing is not to do with wind, not much.
The morning star brings light but little heat—little

light, for that matter, but much hope. Morning and
mourning are so close, so closed within echo.
I would not look into my father's face in the coffin,

but I did see from across the church aisle it was
him within; the light in the church was dim.

Afterward: On *Light Wind Light Light*

More than any of my previous books, this one engages my own actual memory—this at an age, my age, when memory is a radical process, not a passive retreat. I quote Sally Mann: *I tend to agree with the theory that if you want to keep a memory pristine, you must not call upon it too often, for each time it is revisited, you alter it irrevocably, remembering not the original impression left by experience but the last time you recalled it. With tiny differences creeping in at each cycle, the exercise of our memory does not bring us closer to the past but draws us farther away.* (Hold Still: a Memoir with Photographs)

I want poetry, that I write and that I read, to help me become as fully conscious as possible. Poetry is especially helpful in coming to an engagement with the invisible aspects of a world. And so much of this world wants to remain invisible, but invisibilities interact. Light and wind and water engage each other variously as transparent, or at least translucent, thus revelatory, mediums. Qualities of light and transparency figure in some way in every poem in this book, while the book as a whole deals with memory as fluid, transitory, illuminating, and illusionary. We have noticed that the spoon in the water seems to bend, we are all aware that matter can be deceptive.

The sections of this book engage childhood, take steps into the river-like world at large, then return to a transformed version of where the book, and author, began. I marked these boundaries with a primitive numbering system, dots, to emphasize the visual dimension of number—a concern that keeps arising in the collection as the poems ask how abstractions differ from physical sensoria—then ask how perception turns into memory, and what is lost when this happens.

While water does not appear directly in the title, the title otherwise suggests the way language as both object and subject transmutes—the phrase "light light" might consist of an adjective and a noun, for instance. The title resulted from a momentary obsession with the phrases "heavy water," "light wind," and the simple word "light" (for instance as it appears in the Latin phrase in the Old English poem "The Phoenix": *lucis auctor,* "author of light.") Part of the process of any poem is a questioning of the current, immediate implication of each word as it appears in the poem. Heraclitus' image of the river and the unsame-person applies in microcosm to the poem and to the word, any word. The anonymous Old English poet implied light as writing medium, therefore the poet as illuminator, enlightener.

NOTES & ACKNOWLEDGMENTS

First appearances of individual poems:

"The Robe of Ephod, All of Blue," "Spider Mind," and "The Brouwer Fixed-Point Theorem" as "Misunderstanding The Brouwer Fixed-Point Theorem" in *Lana Turner*.

"My Chinese Name" in *Fence*.

"Fall. Things. Sudden (1)," "Theodicy for Beginners," "Visible Is What Others Are, Not What I Can Do" in *Conjunctions*.

"In the Far South the Sun of Autumn Is Passing," "Atmospheric Perspective," and "Enclosure" in *The Colorado Review*.

"Witness: the Modern Sublime" (as "The Modern Sublime"), "Isolating Splendor" (as "Isolated Splendors"), "Tree Names as Folk Etymology" (as "Katsura Tree"), and "To Save Spider and Fly Alike" in *The Volta* (www.thevolta.org/).

"In the Far South the Sun of Autumn Is Passing" *is a line from Wallace Stevens's "Like Decorations in a Nigger Cemetery," and intends to enforce a dialogue with his poem, and with my childhood surrounded by the casual use of that word. Stevens's stanza XXXII is quoted as stanza xi of this poem which also contains crucial borrowings from African-American poets Jean Toomer and Rachel Eliza Griffiths.*

SOURCES:

James Hutton, *THEORY of the EARTH; or an INVESTIGATION of the laws observable in the Composition, Dissolution, and Restoration of Land upon the Globe*, 1788.

Daniel Rockmore, "Objects, Arrows and Rectangles": *In many ways, abstraction in modern art seems to mirror abstraction in mathematics ....At the pinnacle of abstraction sits the subject of "category theory".... In category theory we study "objects" and the "arrows" that transform one object into another.*

Piper Alexis Harron, *The Equidistribution of Lattice Shapes of Rings of Integers of Cubic, Quartic, and Quintic Number Fields: an Artist's Rendering / Based on the original story by Manjul Bhargava and Piper Harron* (Dissertation Presented to the Faculty of Princeton University in Candidacy for the Degree of Doctor of Philosophy, 2015).

Arthur Schopenhauer, *The World as Will and Representation* (1819).

The Institute for Figuring, (founded Los Angeles 2003, destroyed by fire, 2013).

Gregory Benford, "Bow Shock," *Jim Baen's Universe* Vol. 1 No. 1, June 2006.

Suzanne Fierston, "The Beauty of a Map," 1/13/2012 http://blogs.sierra-club.org/explore/art/

Lucretius, *De Rerum Natura, 5. 149-152*

Norbert Elias, *What Is Sociology*, 1978, p. 112.

Michael D. Picone & Amanda LaFleur, *French, in 5 The New Encyclopedia of Southern Culture*: "Language," 60, 63 (Michael Montgomery & Ellen Johnson eds., 2007)

Howard Stein, "Physics and Philosophy Meet: the Strange Case of Poincaré"

Sally Mann, *Hold Still: A Memoir with Photographs*, Little, Brown and Company, 2015

//

"The Robe of Ephod, All of Blue" is for Anna Rabinowitz
"To Save Spider and Fly Alike" is for Beth Nugent
"The Past the Passing" is in memory of Hollis Summers

//

photo by T. Amari

BIN RAMKE grew up in Texas and Louisiana, and lives now in Colorado with Linda and Nic and Ollie.

Light Wind Light Light
by Bin Ramke

Cover art by Moira McDonald: "Origami Boat," Unique lumen photograph (8"x10"). I wanted to make a photograph of how it feels to be floating in a river. So I made an origami boat and as it went down stream, it also made this picture.
www.moiramcdonald.com

Back cover photo by jenelle stafford. www.jeneldorado.com

Text set in Century Gothic and Garamond 3 LT

Cover & Interior Design by Sharon Zetter

Offset printed in the United States
by Edwards Brothers Malloy, Ann Arbor, Michigan
On 55# Enviro Natural 100% Recycled 100% PCW
Acid Free Archival Quality FSC Certified Paper

Publication of this book was made possible in part by gifts from:
The New Place Fund
The Clorox Company Foundation

Omnidawn Publishing
Oakland, California
2018
Rusty Morrison & Ken Keegan, senior editors & co-publishers
Trisha Peck, managing editor & program director
Gillian Olivia Blythe Hamel, senior poetry editor
Cassandra Smith, poetry editor & book designer
Sharon Zetter, poetry editor, book designer & development officer
Liza Flum, poetry editor
Avren Keating, poetry editor & fiction editor
Juliana Paslay, fiction editor
Gail Aronson, fiction editor
Tinia Montford, marketing assistant
Emily Alexander, marketing assistant
Terry A. Taplin, marketing assistant
Matthew Bowie, marketing assistant
SD Sumner, copyeditor